PIANO · VOCAL · GUITAR

THE RETROSPECTIVE COLLECTION

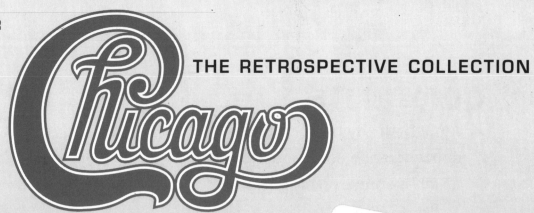

ISBN 0-7935-7076-X

HAL•LEONARD®
CORPORATION
7777 W. BLUEMOUND RD. P.O. BOX 13819 MILWAUKEE, WI 53213

Visit Hal Leonard Online at
www.halleonard.com

CONTENTS
Alphabetically by song title, showing each album on which a song appears.

CONTENTS

**Chronologically by album,
showing the album on which
a song was originally released.**

THE CHICAGO STORY

Like most success stories, Chicago began with a vision.

The place was—where else?—Chicago; the time was the mid 1960s, an era of turbulent change in popular music. Trends came and went swiftly: the British Invasion, blues-rock, bubblegum, acid rock.... In the midst of this turmoil, classically trained clarinet and sax player Walter Parazaider had an idea: a rock 'n' roll band with horns.

Parazaider began assembling his dream group by recruiting guitarist Terry Kath and drummer Danny Seraphine

The Big Thing, 1967. From left: Jimmy Pankow, Robert Lamm, Danny Seraphine (seated), Lee Loughnane, Walt Parazaider, Terry Kath.

from his current band, The Missing Links. For horns, he brought on board two fellow music students from DePaul University: trumpeter Lee Loughnane and trombonist James Pankow. He signed up Robert Lamm, a local piano player, to handle keyboards. The group was formally organized at the kitchen table of Parazaider's apartment in February 1967. By March they were playing gigs. They called themselves The Big Thing.

The Big Thing played throughout the Midwest during the summer of 1967, doing horn-infused covers of popular rock and soul tunes. At an engagement at the end of the summer they ran into Jimmy Guercio, an old musician friend of Parazaider's. Guercio was now a producer for CBS Records, and he liked what he heard in the band. He told them to keep at it, that he'd be in touch. Encouraged by this, Lamm, Kath, and Pankow began writing original material. The next piece of the puzzle fell in place in December, when Peter Cetera joined the group. Not only was he a bass player, but he also sang tenor, and so complemented the baritone voices of lead vocalists Lamm and Kath.

By early 1968 Guercio was preparing to pitch the group to CBS. He renamed them Chicago Transit Authority, or CTA for short, and in June had them pack up and move to Los Angeles. There they wrote continually, practiced incessantly, and played whatever gigs they could, usually for very little money. They played two showcases for CBS West Coast executives, but they were rejected both times. Finally Guercio cut a demo of the group, which caught the ear of CBS president Clive Davis, who overrode the West-Coast veto and signed the group to the Columbia label. In January 1969, the band flew to New York to record their first album.

Chicago Transit Authority hit the market in April 1969. Although AM radio didn't know what to make of it, FM radio—especially college stations—picked up on it immediately. The band quickly garnered a large following on campuses around the country. The album broke onto the *Billboard* Top LP's chart by mid May, reaching a peak of #17. It eventually stayed on that chart for 171 weeks, making it the longest-running album by a rock group at that time. It was certified gold (sales of 500,000 units) by the end of the year, on its way to eventual double-platinum status (over two million sold). In the liner notes of the album they shortened their name to simply Chicago.

In Carnegie Hall, 1971. Danny Seraphine, Walt Parazaider, Jimmy Pankow, Lee Loughnane, Peter Cetera, Robert Lamm, Terry Kath.

The band began touring the U.S., and soon was playing to enthusiastic audiences in Europe. In the meantime, they found time to record their second album. Titled *Chicago II* and released in January 1970, it established the use of the Chicago logo as their album cover art, in what would be a wide variety of treatments through the years, as well as those roman-numeral album titles (Chicago seems to have a thing for numbers, as we shall see). This was also the album that broke Chicago to the public, via AM radio, as a band that produced hit singles.

"Make Me Smile" was the first out of the chute, reaching #9 on the *Billboard* Hot 100. It was followed by "25 or 6 to 4," which made it to #4. Encouraged, Columbia and Chicago decided to try

renewing interest in *Chicago Transit Authority* by releasing a song from that album as a single. It worked; "Does Anybody Really Know What Time It Is?" reached #7.

Chicago III, released at the end of 1970, outsold its predecessor and made it higher on the charts (#2 vs. #4), but its two big singles did only moderately well: "Free" reached #20, "Lowdown" made it to #35. ("Lowdown," written by Cetera and Seraphine, demonstrated the increasing involvement of the members in contributing new songs.) So it was back to the vaults to re-release earlier material. In the summer of '71, "Beginnings," from *CTA*, reached #7 as a two-sided hit; the flip side, "Colour My World," from *Chicago II*, had been paired with "Make Me Smile" a year earlier and had gone nowhere; it now attained the high rank of perennial homecoming and prom theme song. "Questions 67 and 68" (more numbers!), also off of *CTA*, made it to #24 in the fall of 1970, whereas its release two years prior had gotten up to only #71.

The band performed a historic week-long stand at Carnegie Hall in 1971, documenting it with the four-disc album *Chicago IV*. Their next studio project was *Chicago V*, released in July 1972. It was their first album to reach #1 on the charts—setting the pace for the four that followed. It also was the first single-disc Chicago album; *CTA*, *II*, and *III* were all double albums. And it produced the band's first gold single (sales of one million units), "Saturday in the Park." As it turns out, it really was the Fourth of July, in Central Park in New York, to be exact, when Robert Lamm caught the inspiration to write the song. Lamm also wrote "Dialogue (Parts I and II)" for the album, which became a big hit as sung by Kath and Cetera.

Jimmy Guercio remained an influential force in the life of the band. He continued to produce their albums and built a recording studio in Colorado, dubbed the Caribou Ranch, where Chicago would cut the remainder of the albums they made with him. During a break from touring in support of *Chicago V*, several members of the band contributed performances (musical and dramatic) to a movie Guercio produced and directed, *Electra Glide in Blue*.

James Pankow wrote two Top 10 hits for *Chicago VI*, released in mid 1973. The first was "Feelin' Stronger Every Day," and the second was the romantic ballad "Just You 'n' Me," which foreshadowed the direction in which the band would find success in coming years. Pankow was on a roll. His "(I've Been) Searchin' So Long" was the first single off *Chicago VII* in early 1974. That was followed by "Call On Me," which was trumpeter Lee Loughnane's first attempt at writing

Circa 1976. Back row: Danny Seraphine, Laudir de Oliveira, Lee Loughnane, Terry Kath. Front row: Peter Cetera, Walt Parazaider, Jimmy Pankow, Robert Lamm.

for the group. Both made the Top 10. The third single off the album was Cetera's "Wishing You Were Here," in which he got to realize his dream of singing with the Beach Boys. The two groups had such a good time in the studio that they toured the U.S. together that summer, packing stadiums wherever they went. During 1974 Chicago also expanded its membership to eight by adding percussionist Laudir de Oliveira. De Oliveira had first played with the group as a sideman on *Chicago VI*.

Chicago VIII, released at the beginning of 1975, spawned a number of hit singles, most notably "Harry Truman" and "Old Days." The greatest-hits *Chicago IX* followed later that year, becoming the

group's fifth #1 album in a row. *Chicago X* came out in the summer of 1976, yielding the Top 40 hit "Another Rainy Day in New York City" and "If You Leave Me Now," written and sung by Peter Cetera. That song became the group's first #1 single.

The group's momentum continued with *Chicago XI* in the fall of 1977 and the hit single "Baby What a Big Surprise." But then everything changed. First the band split with Jimmy Guercio. Then came the death of Terry Kath in January 1978 from an accidental gunshot wound. The members of the band found a new producer in Phil Ramone (no relation to the band The Ramones), hired a new guitarist in Donnie Dacus, and marked the beginning of a new era by giving their next album an individual title—*Hot Streets*—and putting a photo of the band on the cover, rather than the familiar logo.

Hot Streets, which was released in September 1978, was certified platinum by the end of October. It produced two Top 20 singles: "No Tell Lover" and the up-tempo "Alive Again," in which Chicago asserted its commitment to go on. Despite this commitment, the next few years were difficult ones. *Chicago XIII*, which attempted to come to terms with the disco trend of the day, suffered from poor sales, at least by Chicago standards. It also marked the end of the group's short-lived relationships with Phil Ramone and Donnie Dacus.

Chris Pinnick was hired as a sideman to replace Dacus, and Tom Dowd was brought in to produce *Chicago XIV*. Released in July 1980, it also fared poorly in sales. Furthermore, its only hit single,

"Thunder and Lightning," peaked at a disappointing #56. Columbia bought out the remainder of the band's recording contract and released a greatest-hits album as *Chicago XV*. Laudir de Oliveira also left the band at this point.

In 1982, Chicago started with a new record label, the Full Moon division of Warner Brothers, and achieved new commercial success with the album *Chicago 16*. They accomplished this by going with what Chicago audiences liked best: ballads sung by Peter Cetera. "Hard to Say I'm Sorry" shot to #1 and went gold. The album itself made the Top 10, which the band hadn't seen since *Chicago XI* in 1977. Part of the success of *Chicago 16* (by the way, note the break with the past by the use of arabic, rather than roman, numerals) lay in the skillful production work of David Foster. Foster, in turn, was introduced to Chicago by their newest member, Bill Champlin, who sang and also handled guitar and keyboard duties.

The followup album, *Chicago 17*, became the group's biggest album ever, selling over six million copies. It reached #4 on the charts and yielded the Top 5 hits "Hard Habit to Break" and "You're the Inspiration." With this series of romantic ballads, the spotlight was becoming more tightly focused on the singing and songwriting of Peter Cetera. He decided at the end of the group's summer 1985 tour that the time was ripe for a solo career. Jason Scheff replaced him with both tenor vocals and bass playing on *Chicago 18*, released in September 1986. His big test came with "Will You Still Love Me," and he passed it admirably, taking the song to #3.

A period of experimentation with material followed. *Chicago 19* (1988) included two big hits by songwriter Diane Warren: "Look Away" (which rocketed to #1) and "I Don't Wanna Live without Your Love." Following *Chicago 20: Greatest Hits 1982–1989*, the band scored with two more of Warren's songs on *Chicago Twenty 1*: "Explain It to My Heart" and "Chasin' the Wind." Several different producers were used on these albums, and band membership changed a few times: guitarist DaWayne Bailey came and went, and founding drummer Danny Seraphine left the group, to be replaced by Tris Imboden. But one thing that solidified during this unsettled period was a return of the horns to the forefront of the band.

In 1993 Chicago recorded *The Stone of Sisyphus* with producer Peter Wolf. Warner Brothers and the band disagreed about the album and parted ways. *Sisyphus* remains unreleased as of this writing. In 1995 the group secured the rights to their recordings for Columbia and re-released them on their own Chicago Records label. They also moved to Giant Records for the recording of *Night & Day*. The new album, with Bruce Fairbairn producing, "Chicago-ized" big-band standards such as "Caravan" and "In the Mood." It was a further extension of the central role the horns played in the Chicago sound.

Since the release of that album, Chicago made guitarist Keith Howland its latest member, embarked on a series of performances with symphony orchestras, and released an "ultimate greatest hits" package, *The Heart of Chicago 1967–1997* on Reprise Records. As the band marks its thirtieth anniversary, it keeps moving forward, guided by what started it all: a vision.

Chicago in 1995. Bill Champlin, Robert Lamm, Walt Parazaider (rear), Lee Loughnane, Tris Imboden, James Pankow, Jason Scheff.

CHICAGO TRANSIT AUTHORITY
(Columbia, 1969)

Personnel

Chicago: Robert Lamm (Keyboards, Vocals), Terry Kath (Guitar, Vocals), Peter Cetera (Bass, Vocals), Lee Loughnane (Trumpet, Background Vocals), James Pankow (Trombone), Walter Parazaider (Woodwinds, Background Vocals), Danny Seraphine (Drums) • *Producer:* James William Guercio

Songs

Introduction • Does Anybody Really Know What Time It Is? • Beginnings • Questions 67 and 68 • Listen • Poem 58 • Free Form Guitar • South California Purples • I'm a Man • Prologue, August 29, 1968 • Someday (August 29, 1968) • Liberation

CHICAGO II (Columbia, 1970)

Personnel

Chicago: Robert Lamm (Keyboards, Vocals), Terry Kath (Guitar, Vocals), Peter Cetera (Bass, Vocals), Lee Loughnane (Trumpet, Background Vocals), James Pankow (Trombone), Walter Parazaider (Woodwinds, Background Vocals), Danny Seraphine (Drums) • *Producer:* James William Guercio

Songs

Movin' In • The Road • Poem for the People • In the Country • Wake Up Sunshine • Make Me Smile • So Much to Say, So Much to Give • Anxiety's Moment • West Virginia Fantasies • Colour My World • To Be Free • Now More Than Ever • Fancy Colours • 25 or 6 to 4 • Prelude • A.M. Mourning • P.M. Mourning • Memories of Love • It Better End Soon: 1st Movement • 2nd Movement • 3rd Movement • 4th Movement • Where Do We Go from Here

CHICAGO III (Columbia, 1970)

Personnel

Chicago: Robert Lamm (Keyboards, Vocals), Terry Kath (Guitar, Vocals), Peter Cetera (Bass, Vocals), Lee Loughnane (Trumpet, Background Vocals), James Pankow (Trombone), Walter Parazaider (Woodwinds, Background Vocals), Danny Seraphine (Drums) • *Producer:* James William Guercio

Songs

Sing a Mean Tune Kid • Loneliness Is Just a Word • What Else Can I Say • I Don't Want Your Money • Flight 602 • Motorboat to Mars • Free • Free Country • At the Sunrise • Happy 'Cause I'm Going Home • Mother • Lowdown • A Hard Risin' Morning without Breakfast • Off to Work • Fallin' Out • Dreamin' Home • Morning Blues Again • When All the Laughter Dies in Sorrow • Canon • Once upon a Time… • Progress? • Approaching Storm • Man vs. Man: The End

CHICAGO IV: LIVE AT CARNEGIE HALL
(Columbia, 1971)

Personnel

Chicago: Robert Lamm (Keyboards, Vocals), Terry Kath (Guitar, Vocals), Peter Cetera (Bass, Vocals), Lee Loughnane (Trumpet, Background Vocals, Percussion, Guitar), James Pankow (Trombone, Percussion), Walter Parazaider (Woodwinds, Percussion, Background Vocals), Danny Seraphine (Drums) • *Producer:* James William Guercio

Songs

In the Country • Fancy Colours • Does Anybody Really Know What Time It Is? • South California Purples • Questions 67 and 68 • Sing a Mean Tune Kid • Beginnings • It Better End Soon: 1st Movement • 2nd Movement • 3rd Movement • 4th Movement • 5th Movement • Intro • Mother • Lowdown • Flight 602 • Motorboat to Mars • Free • Where Do We Go from Here • I Don't Want Your Money • Happy 'Cause I'm Home • Ballet for a Girl in Buchannon • Make Me Smile • So Much to Say, So Much to Give • Anxiety's Moment • West Virginia Fantasies • Colour My World • To Be Free • Now More Than Ever • A Song for Richard and His Friends • 25 or 6 to 4 • I'm a Man

CHICAGO V (Columbia, 1972)

Personnel

Chicago: Robert Lamm (Keyboards, Vocals), Terry Kath (Guitar, Vocals), Peter Cetera (Bass, Vocals), Lee Loughnane (Trumpet, Background Vocals, Percussion), James Pankow (Trombone, Percussion), Walter Parazaider (Woodwinds, Percussion), Danny Seraphine (Drums, Percussion) • *Producer:* James William Guercio

Songs

A Hit by Varese • All Is Well • Now That You've Gone • Dialogue (Part I) • Dialogue (Part II) • While the City Sleeps • Saturday in the Park • State of the Union • Goodbye • Alma Mater

CHICAGO VI (Columbia, 1973)

Personnel

Chicago: Robert Lamm (Keyboards, Vocals), Terry Kath (Guitar, Vocals), Peter Cetera (Bass, Vocals), Lee Loughnane (Trumpet, Background Vocals), James Pankow (Trombone), Walter Parazaider (Woodwinds, Background Vocals), Danny Seraphine (Drums) • *Additional Musicians:* Laudir de Oliveira (Percussion), Joe Lala (Percussion), J.G. O'Rafferty (Pedal Steel Guitar) • *Producer:* James William Guercio

Songs

Critics' Choice • Just You 'n' Me • Darlin' Dear • Jenny • What's This World Comin' To • Something in This City Changes People • Hollywood • In Terms of Two • Rediscovery • Feelin' Stronger Every Day

CHICAGO VII (Columbia, 1974)

Personnel

Chicago: Robert Lamm (Keyboards, Vocals), Terry Kath (Guitar, Bass, Percussion, Vocals), Peter Cetera (Bass, Guitar, Vocals), Lee Loughnane (Trumpet, Flugelhorn, Vocals), James Pankow (Trombone, Percussion, Vocals), Walter Parazaider (Woodwinds), Danny Seraphine (Drums, Percussion) • *Additional Musicians:* Alan Jardine (Vocals), Carl Wilson (Vocals), Dennis Wilson (Vocals), The Pointer Sisters (Vocals), David J. Wolinski (Keyboards), Wayne Tarnowski (Keyboards), James William Guercio (Guitar, Bass), Ross Salomone (Drums), Guille Garcia (Percussion) • *Producer:* James William Guercio

Songs

Prelude to Aire • Aire • Devil's Sweet • Italian from New York • Hanky Panky • Life Saver • Happy Man • (I've Been) Searchin' So Long • Mongonucleosis • Song of the Evergreens • Byblos • Wishing You Were Here • Call On Me • Woman Don't Want to Love Me • Skinny Boy

CHICAGO VIII (Columbia, 1975)

Personnel

Chicago: Robert Lamm (Keyboards, Vocals), Terry Kath (Guitar, Vocals), Peter Cetera (Bass, Vocals), Lee Loughnane (Trumpet, Vocals), James Pankow (Trombone), Walter Parazaider (Woodwinds), Danny Seraphine (Drums), Laudir de Oliveira (Percussion) • *Additional Musicians:* The Caribou Kitchenettes (Vocals) • *Producer:* James William Guercio

Songs

Anyway You Want • Brand New Love Affair—Pt. I / Brand New Love Affair—Pt. II • Never Been In Love Before • Hideaway • Till We Meet Again • Harry Truman • Oh, Thank You Great Spirit • Long Time No See • Ain't It Blue? • Old Days

CHICAGO IX: CHICAGO'S GREATEST HITS (Columbia, 1975)

Personnel

Chicago: Robert Lamm (Keyboards, Vocals), Terry Kath (Guitar, Vocals), Peter Cetera (Bass, Vocals), Lee Loughnane (Trumpet, Vocals), James Pankow (Trombone), Walter Parazaider (Woodwinds), Danny Seraphine (Drums), Laudir de Oliveira (Percussion) • *Producer:* James William Guercio

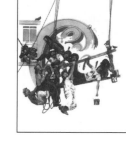

Songs

25 or 6 to 4 • Does Anybody Really Know What Time It Is? • Colour My World • Just You 'n' Me • Saturday in the Park • Feelin' Stronger Every Day • Make Me Smile • Wishing You Were Here • Call On Me • (I've Been) Searchin' So Long • Beginnings

CHICAGO X (Columbia, 1976)

Personnel

Chicago: Robert Lamm (Keyboards, Vocals), Terry Kath (Guitar, Vocals), Peter Cetera (Bass, Vocals), Lee Loughnane (Trumpet, Vocals), James Pankow (Trombone, Vocals), Walter Parazaider (Woodwinds, Vocals), Danny Seraphine (Drums, Vocals), Laudir de Oliveira (Percussion, Vocals) • *Additional Musicians:* David J. Wolinski (Keyboards), James William Guercio (Guitar, Bass), Othello Molineaux (Steel Drums), Leroy Williams (Steel Drums) • *Producer:* James William Guercio

Songs

Once or Twice • You Are On My Mind • Skin Tight • If You Leave Me Now • Together Again • Another Rainy Day in New York City • Mama Mama • Scrapbook • Gently I'll Wake You • You Get It Up • Hope for Love

CHICAGO XI (Columbia, 1977)

Personnel

Chicago: Robert Lamm (Keyboards, Percussion, Vocals), Terry Kath (Guitar, Percussion, Vocals), Peter Cetera (Bass, Vocals), Lee Loughnane (Trumpet, Flugelhorn, Vocals), James Pankow (Trombone, Keyboards, Percussion, Vocals), Walter Parazaider (Woodwinds), Danny Seraphine (Drums, Percussion), Laudir de Oliveira (Percussion) • *Additional Musicians:* Tim Cetera (Vocals), Carl Wilson (Vocals), Chaka Khan (Vocals), The Voices of Inspiration (Vocals), David "Hawk" Wolinski (Keyboards), James William Guercio (Guitar, Bass) • *Producer:* James William Guercio

Songs

Mississippi Delta City Blues • Baby What a Big Surprise • Till the End of Time • Policeman • Take Me Back to Chicago • Vote for Me • Takin' It On Uptown • This Time • Inner Struggles of a Man • Prelude • Little One

HOT STREETS (Columbia, 1978)

Personnel

Chicago: Robert Lamm (Keyboards, Vocals), Donnie Dacus (Guitar), Peter Cetera (Bass, Vocals), Lee Loughnane (Trumpet, Vocals), James Pankow (Trombone), Walter Parazaider (Woodwinds), Danny Seraphine (Drums), Laudir de Oliveira (Percussion) • *Producer:* Phil Ramone

Songs

Alive Again • Greatest Love on Earth • Little Miss Lovin' • Hot Streets • Take a Chance • Gone Long Gone • Ain't It Time • Love Was New • No Tell Lover • Show Me the Way

CHICAGO XIII (Columbia, 1979)

Personnel

Chicago: Robert Lamm (Keyboards, Vocals), Donnie Dacus (Guitar), Peter Cetera (Bass, Vocals), Lee Loughnane (Trumpet, Vocals), James Pankow (Trombone), Walter Parazaider (Woodwinds), Danny Seraphine (Drums), Laudir de Oliveira (Percussion) • *Additional Musicians:* Maynard Ferguson (Trumpet), Airto Moreira (Percussion), David "Hawk" Wolinski (Synthesizer) • *Producer:* Phil Ramone

Songs

Street Player • Mama Take • Must Have Been Crazy • Window Dreamin' • Paradise Alley • Aloha Mama • Returns • Loser with a Broken Heart • Life Is What It Is • Run Away

CHICAGO XIV (Columbia, 1980)

Personnel

Chicago: Robert Lamm (Keyboards, Vocals), Peter Cetera (Bass, Vocals), Lee Loughnane (Trumpet, Vocals), James Pankow (Trombone), Walter Parazaider (Woodwinds), Danny Seraphine (Drums), Laudir de Oliveira (Percussion) • *Additional Musicians:* Chris Pinnick (Guitar) • *Producer:* Tom Dowd

Songs

Manipulation • Upon Arrival • Song for You • Where Did the Lovin' Go • Birthday Boy • Hold On • Overnight Cafe • Thunder and Lightning • I'd Rather Be Rich • The American Dream

CHICAGO XV: GREATEST HITS VOLUME II (Columbia, 1981)

Personnel

Chicago: Robert Lamm (Keyboards, Vocals), Terry Kath (Guitar, Vocals), Donnie Dacus (Guitar), Peter Cetera (Bass, Vocals), Lee Loughnane (Trumpet, Vocals), James Pankow (Trombone), Walter Parazaider (Woodwinds), Danny Seraphine (Drums), Laudir de Oliveira (Percussion) • *Producers:* James William Guercio, Phil Ramone, Chicago

Songs

Baby What a Big Surprise • Dialogue (Part II) • No Tell Lover • Alive Again • Old Days • If You Leave Me Now • Questions 67 and 68 • Happy Man • Gone Long Gone • Take Me Back to Chicago

CHICAGO 16
(Full Moon/Warner, 1982)

Personnel

Chicago: Robert Lamm (Keyboards, Vocals), Bill Champlin (Guitar, Keyboards, Vocals), Peter Cetera (Bass, Vocals), Lee Loughnane (Trumpet, Vocals), James Pankow (Trombone), Walter Parazaider (Woodwinds), Danny Seraphine (Drums) • *Additional Musicians:* David Foster (Keyboards), Chris Pinnick (Guitar), Michael Landau (Guitar), Steve Lukather (Guitar) • *Producer:* David Foster

Songs

What You're Missing • Waiting for You to Decide • Bad Advice • Chains • Hard to Say I'm Sorry • Get Away • Follow Me • Sonny Think Twice • What Can I Say • Rescue You • Love Me Tomorrow

CHICAGO 17 (Warner Bros., 1984)

Personnel

Chicago: Robert Lamm (Keyboards, Vocals), Bill Champlin (Guitar, Keyboards, Vocals), Peter Cetera (Bass, Vocals), Lee Loughnane (Trumpet), James Pankow (Trombone), Walter Parazaider (Woodwinds), Danny Seraphine (Drums) • *Additional Musicians:* David Foster (Keyboards), Chris Pinnick (Guitar), Michael Landau (Guitar), Paul Jackson (Guitar), Mark Goldenberg (Guitar), Ken Cetera (Vocals), Donny Osmond (Vocals), Richard Marx (Vocals), Gary Grant (Trumpet), Greg Adams (Trumpet), Paulinho da Costa (Percussion) • *Producer:* David Foster

Songs

Stay the Night • We Can Stop the Hurtin' • Hard Habit to Break • Only You • Remember the Feeling • Along Comes a Woman • You're the Inspiration • Please Hold On • Prima Donna • Once in a Lifetime

CHICAGO 18
(Full Moon/Warner, 1986)

Personnel

Chicago: Robert Lamm (Keyboards, Vocals), Bill Champlin (Keyboards, Vocals), Jason Scheff (Bass, Vocals), Lee Loughnane (Trumpet), James Pankow (Trombone), Walter Parazaider (Woodwinds), Danny Seraphine (Drums) • *Additional Musicians:* David Foster (Keyboards), Michael Landau (Guitar), Buzz Feiten (Guitar), Steve Lukather (Guitar) • *Producer:* David Foster

Songs

Niagara Falls • Forever • If She Would Have Been Faithful • 25 or 6 to 4 • Will You Still Love Me • Over and Over • It's Alright • Nothin's Gonna Stop Us Now • I Believe • One More Day

CHICAGO 19 (Warner Bros., 1988)

Personnel

Chicago: Robert Lamm (Keyboards, Vocals), Bill Champlin (Keyboards, Vocals), Jason Scheff (Bass, Vocals), Lee Loughnane (Trumpet), James Pankow (Trombone), Walter Parazaider (Saxophone), Danny Seraphine (Drums, Percussion) • *Additional Musicians:* Tim Feehan (Vocals), Tamara Champlin (Vocals), Charles Judge (Keyboards), Kiki Ebsen (Keyboards), John Campbell (Keyboards), Philip Ashley (Keyboards), DaWayne Bailey (Guitar, Vocals), Dan Huff (Guitar), Chas Sandford (Guitar), Mike Murphy (Percussion) • *Producers:* Chas Sandford, Ron Nevison

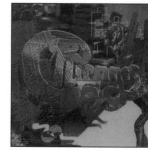

Songs

Heart in Pieces • I Don't Wanna Live without Your Love • I Stand Up • We Can Last Forever • Come In from the Night • Look Away • What Kind of Man Would I Be? • Runaround • You're Not Alone • Victorious

CHICAGO 20: GREATEST HITS 1982–1989
(Warner Bros., 1989)

Personnel

Chicago: Robert Lamm (Keyboards, Vocals), Bill Champlin (Guitar, Keyboards, Vocals), Peter Cetera (Bass, Vocals), Jason Scheff (Bass, Vocals), Lee Loughnane (Trumpet, Flugelhorn, Vocals), James Pankow (Trombone, Vocals), Walter Parazaider (Woodwinds, Vocals), Danny Seraphine (Drums) • *Additional Musicians:* David Foster (Keyboards), Robbie Buchanan (Keyboards), Tom Keane (Keyboards), Steve Porcaro (Keyboards), Efrain Toro (Keyboards), DaWayne Bailey (Guitar, Vocals), Michael Landau (Guitar), Steve "Doc" Kupka (Horn), John Keane (Drums) • *Producers:* David Foster, Ron Nevison, Chas Sandford

Songs

Hard to Say I'm Sorry/Get Away • Look Away • Stay the Night • Will You Still Love Me • Love Me Tomorrow • What Kind of Man Would I Be? (Remix) • You're the Inspiration • I Don't Wanna Live without Your Love • Hard Habit to Break • Along Comes a Woman • If She Would Have Been Faithful • We Can Last Forever

CHICAGO TWENTY 1
(Warner Bros., 1992)

Personnel

Chicago: Robert Lamm (Keyboards, Vocals), Bill Champlin (Keyboards, Vocals), DaWayne Bailey (Guitar, Vocals), Jason Scheff (Bass, Vocals), Lee Loughnane (Trumpet, Flugelhorn, Vocals), James Pankow (Trombone, Vocals), Walter Parazaider (Woodwinds, Vocals) • *Additional Musicians:* Robbie Buchanan (Keyboards), Efrain Toro (Keyboards), Tom Keane (Keyboards), David Foster (Piano), Michael Landau (Guitar), Stephen "Doc" Kupka (Horn), Tris Imboden (Drums), John Keane (Drums) • *Producers:* Ron Nevison, Humberto Gatica

Songs

Explain It to My Heart • If It Were You • You Come to My Senses • Somebody, Somewhere • What Does It Take • One from the Heart • Chasin' the Wind • God Save the Queen • Man to Woman • Only Time Can Heal the Wounded • Who Do You Love • Holdin' On

NIGHT & DAY: BIG BAND
(Giant Records, 1995)

Personnel

Chicago: Robert Lamm (Keyboards, Vocals), Bill Champlin (Keyboards, Guitar, Vocals), Jason Scheff (Bass, Vocals), Lee Loughnane (Trumpet, Flugelhorn), James Pankow (Trombone), Walter Parazaider (Winds), Tris Imboden (Drums, Harmonica) • *Additional Musicians:* The Gipsy Kings (Vocals), Jade (Vocals), Paul Shaffer (Piano), Bruce Gaitsch (Guitar), Joe Perry (Guitar), Luis Conte (Percussion), Jack Duncan (Percussion), Sal Ferreras (Percussion) • *Producer:* Bruce Fairbairn

Songs

Chicago • Caravan • Dream a Little Dream of Me • Goody Goody • Moonlight Serenade • Night & Day • Blues in the Night • Sing, Sing, Sing • Sophisticated Lady • In the Mood • Don't Get Around Much Anymore • Take the "A" Train

THE HEART OF CHICAGO 1967–1997
(Reprise Records, 1997)

Personnel

Chicago: Robert Lamm [Keyboards, Vocals], Lee Loughnane [Trumpet], James Pankow [Trombone], Walter Parazaider [Winds], Bill Champlin [Keyboards, Guitar, Vocals], Jason Scheff [Bass, Vocals], Tris Imboden [Drums], Keith Howland [Guitar] • *Producers:* David Foster, James William Guercio, Lenny Kravitz, Ron Nevison, James Newton Howard

Songs

You're the Inspiration • If You Leave Me Now • Make Me Smile • Hard Habit to Break • Saturday in the Park • Wishing You Were Here • The Only One • Colour My World • Look Away • Here in My Heart • Just You 'n' Me • Does Anybody Really Know What Time It Is? • Will You Still Love Me • Beginnings • Hard to Say I'm Sorry/Get Away

ALIVE AGAIN

Words and Music by
JAMES PANKOW

ANOTHER RAINY DAY IN NEW YORK CITY

Words and Music by
ROBERT LAMM

BABY WHAT A BIG SURPRISE

Words and Music by
PETER CETERA

BEGINNINGS

Words and Music by
ROBERT LAMM

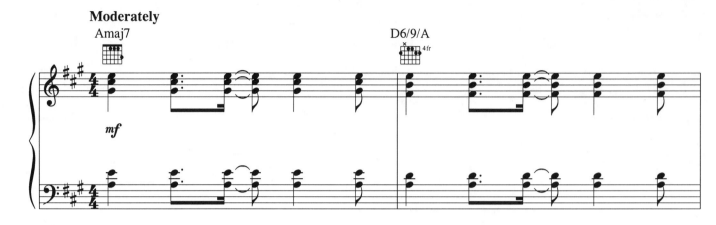

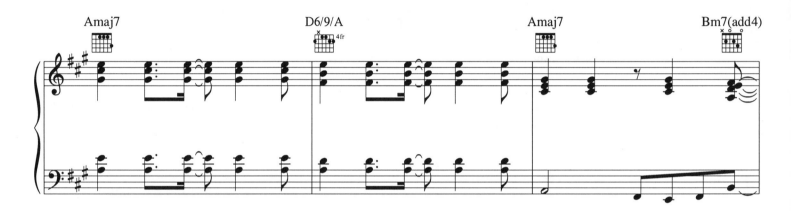

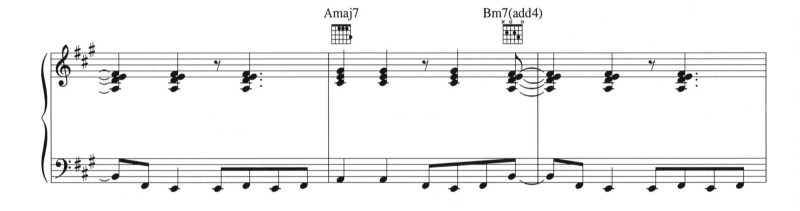

When I'm with ___ you, _____ it does-n't mat -

When I kiss ___ you, _____ I feel a thou -

ter where we are _____ or what we're do - in'. _____

sand dif-f'rent feel - ings, the col - or of chills _____

CALL ON ME

Words and Music by
LEE LOUGHNANE

CARAVAN

Words and Music by DUKE ELLINGTON,
IRVING MILLS and JUAN TIZOL

Bright Latin beat

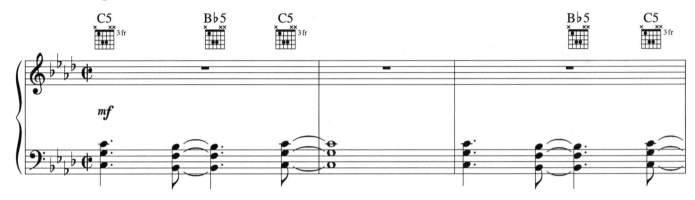

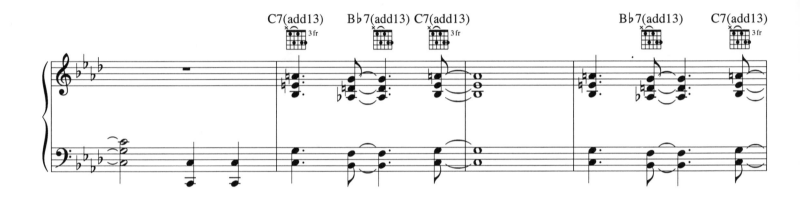

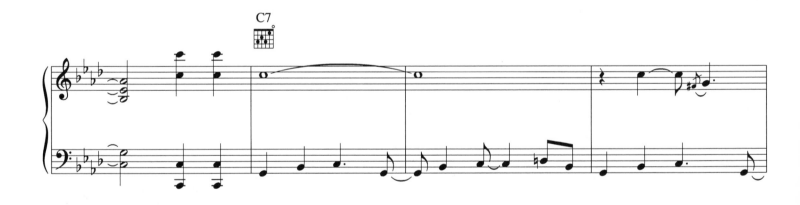

our car - a - van.

our car - a - van.

Solo ends

This _____

_____ is so ex - cit - ing.

You _____ are so in - vit - ing,

Oh. _____

COLOUR MY WORLD

Words and Music by
JAMES PANKOW

As time goes on, _____ I re-al-

DOES ANYBODY REALLY KNOW WHAT TIME IT IS?

Words and Music by
ROBERT LAMM

As I was walk - ing down _ the street _ one day, _
And I was walk - ing down _ the street _ one day.
And I was walk - ing down _ the street _ one day, _

DIALOGUE (PART I)

Words and Music by
ROBERT LAMM

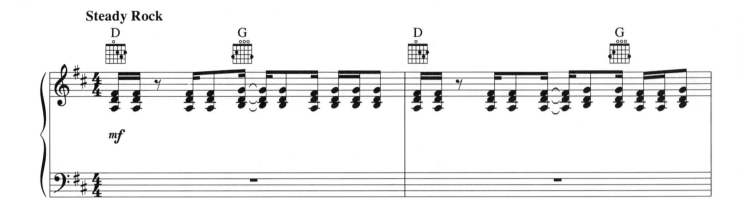

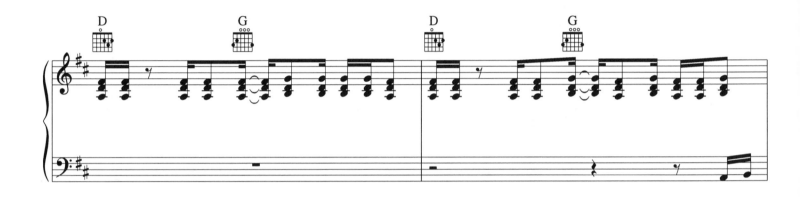

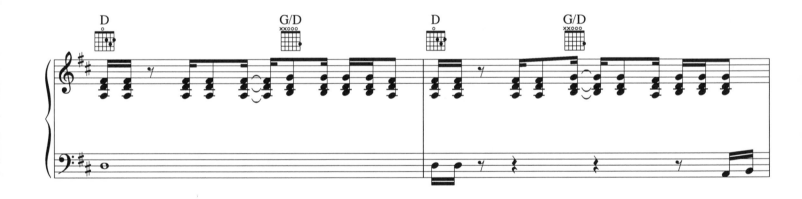

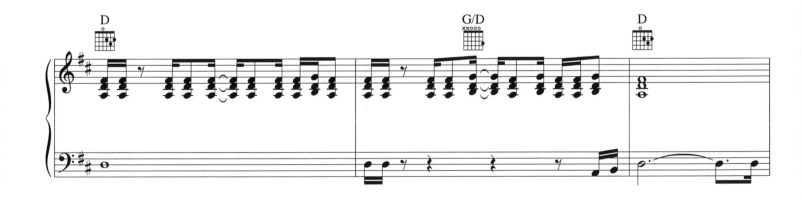

Thank you for __ the talk, __ you know, __ you

DIALOGUE (PART II)

Words and Music by
ROBERT LAMM

I DON'T WANNA LIVE WITHOUT YOUR LOVE

Words and Music by DIANE WARREN
and ALBERT HAMMOND

FEELIN' STRONGER EVERY DAY

Words and Music by PETER CETERA
and JAMES PANKOW

FREE

Words and Music by
ROBERT LAMM

HARD HABIT TO BREAK

Words and Music by JOHN LEWIS PARKER
and STEPHEN KIPNER

Moderately slow

MCA music publishing

HARD TO SAY I'M SORRY

Words and Music by PETER CETERA
and DAVID FOSTER

HARRY TRUMAN

Words and Music by
ROBERT LAMM

Moderate Rock

mf

A - mer - i - ca needs _ you,

Har - ry Tru - man. ___ Har - ry, could you please come home? ___

Things are look - in' bad. ___ I know you would be mad ___ to

Oh, __ whoa, _ whoa. _

D.S. al Coda

A -

IF SHE WOULD HAVE BEEN FAITHFUL

Words and Music by STEVE KIPNER
and RANDY GOODRUM

IF YOU LEAVE ME NOW

Words and Music by
PETER CETERA

D.S. al Coda
(with repeats)

Ooh, _____ girl, _____ just
Ooh, ma - ma, _____ I just

got to have _ you by _ my side. _____
got to have _ your lov - in'. _____

Repeat and Fade

Ooh, _____

JUST YOU 'N' ME

Words and Music by
JAMES PANKOW

Love me to-night, ___ love me for-ev - er, and ev-
- er. ___

LOOK AWAY

Words and Music by
DIANE WARREN

LOWDOWN

Words and Music by PETER CETERA
and DANNY SERAPHINE

Oh, __

Guitar solo - ad lib.

Solo ends

MAKE ME SMILE

Words and Music by
JAMES PANKOW

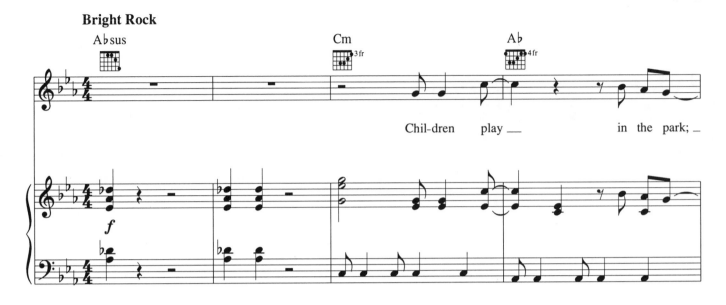

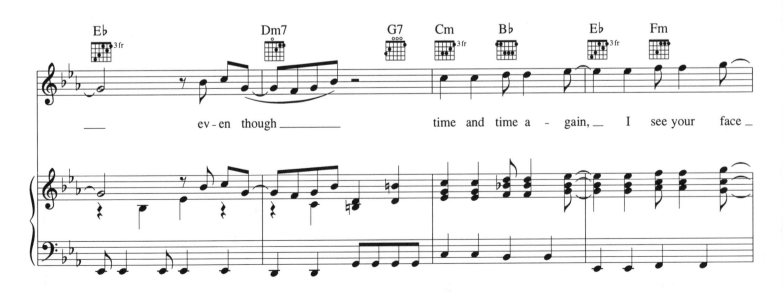

when I hold ___ you, _____ cry sweet tears of joy, ___ touch the sky. _
we're to - geth - er. _____ Tell me you will stay; _

NO TELL LOVER

Words and Music by LEE LOUGHNANE,
DANNY SERAPHINE and PETER CETERA

OLD DAYS

Words and Music by
JAMES PANKOW

QUESTIONS 67 AND 68

Words and Music by
ROBERT LAMM

Slow Rock ballad

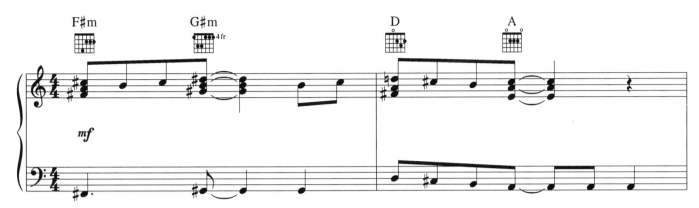

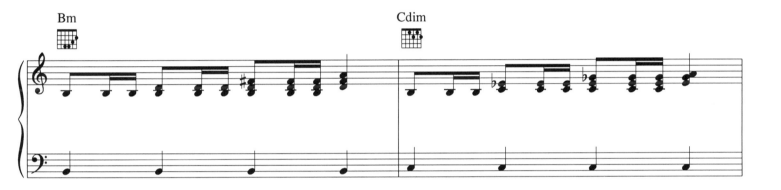

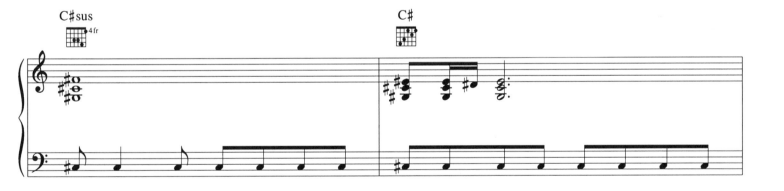

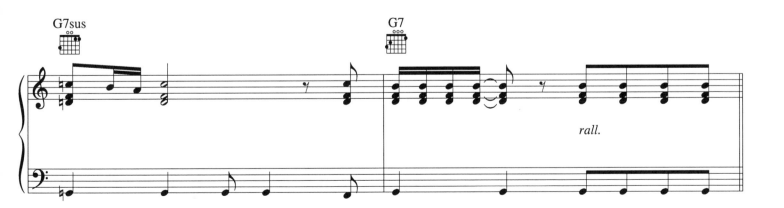

Ques - tions six - ty - sev - en and six - ty - eight.

SATURDAY IN THE PARK

Words and Music by
ROBERT LAMM

THUNDER AND LIGHTNING

Words and Music by ROBERT LAMM,
DANIEL SERAPHINE and PETER CETERA

(Brass)

I thought   that you _____ thought   that _____ we _____
Thun - der   and   light - ning,   and _____ you _____
It hurt   to   see _____ you   play _____ games _____

(I'VE BEEN)
SEARCHIN' SO LONG

Words and Music by
JAMES PANKOW

25 OR 6 TO 4

Words and Music by
ROBERT LAMM

Bright Rock

WHAT KIND OF MAN WOULD I BE?

Words and Music by JASON SCHEFF,
CHAS SANDFORD and BOBBY CALDWELL

know you could sure-ly ___ sur-vive with-out me. But if I had to live ___ with-out ___

___ you, ___ tell me what kind of man, ___ tell ___ me

what kind of man, ___ tell ___ me what kind ___ of man ___ would ___ I ___

Repeat and Fade

be?
What kind ___ of man would ___ I ___ be?

Tell ___ me

WILL YOU STILL LOVE ME

Words and Music by RICHARD BASKIN,
TOM KEANE and DAVID FOSTER

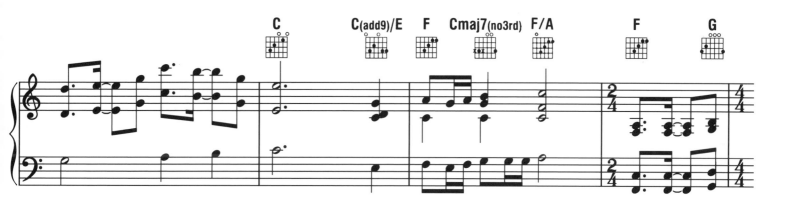

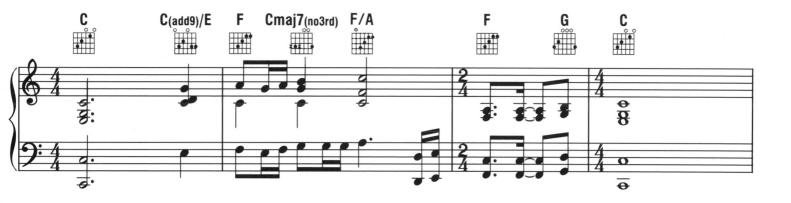

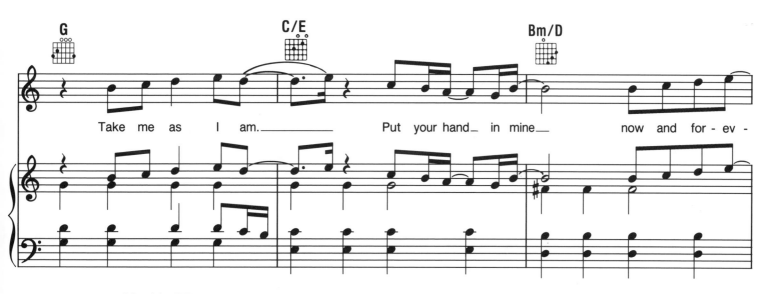

Take me as I am._____ Put your hand__ in mine__ now and for-ev-

MCA music publishing

WISHING YOU WERE HERE

Words and Music by
PETER CETERA

YOU'RE NOT ALONE

By JIMMY SCOTT

I see you there, a sil-hou-ette in the moon-light.
Pools of sor-row and tears of joy.

Looks like you've giv-en up on love.
There's a bro-ken-up girl for ev-'ry bro-ken-down boy,

YOU'RE THE INSPIRATION

Words and Music by PETER CETERA
and DAVID FOSTER

Additional Lyrics

2. And I know (yes, I know)
   That it's plain to see
   We're so in love when we're together.
   Now I know (now I know)
   That I need you here with me
   From tonight until the end of time.
   You should know everywhere I go;
   Always on my mind, you're in my heart, in my soul.
   (To Chorus:)